W9-BUV-782

E CLI
Cline-Ransome, Lesa
Benny Goodman & Teddy Wilson :
taking the stage …

DATE DUE			

Middletown Library Service Center
786 South Main Street
Middletown, CT 06457

Benny Goodman & Teddy Wilson

Taking the Stage as the First Black-and-White Jazz Band in History

by **Lesa Cline-Ransome** • Illustrated by **James E. Ransome**

Middletown Library Service Center
786 South Main Street
Middletown, CT 06457

Holiday House / New York

Chicago's West Side Colt's Electric Park, 1922

Pop boom pop boom
Above Benny,
the Fourth of July exploded
One hundred colors, loud,
live and hot
In front of him, the jazz band
clarinet, piano, drums
pop boom pop boom
Benny sat, toe tapping,
fingers snapping,
listening

Tuskegee, Alabama
Tuskegee College, 1926

Outside Teddy's window, birds sang
Tweet drum chirp tweet drum chirp
Inside on the gramophone
Records spinning, needles scratching,
horns blowing
Duke Ellington, Fats Waller,
Earl Hines on piano
Light as a feather
ting ping tap ting ping tap
Teddy stood, toe tapping,
fingers snapping,
Listening

Benny walked down Maxwell Street
With his brothers and dad
Past streetcars, around peddlers, away from gang fights
into free concerts, lessons and music
with the synagogue marching band
one instrument for each brother
largest to smallest
a tuba for Harry
a trumpet for Freddy
a clarinet for Benny

Dirt roads, farms and classrooms
Letters, books, pride
and music
filled Teddy and his brother
Trombone for Gus
Violin, oboe, clarinet and
Piano for Teddy

Benny practiced
when the kids were outside playing
when his mother called him to supper
when everyone was trying to sleep
the music from his tutor
from sheets of German music
Tight, *toot*, formal, *toot*
Noone, Dodds,
New Orleans Rhythm Kings
Black and blues, mellow and loose

Teddy practiced
Reeds and brass
recitals and concerts
Reading bass and treble clefs
With his tutor
Ping, overtures, *ping*, études, Chopin, Bach
But Duke, Fats and Hines
he copied note by note
Black and blues, mellow and loose

Onstage
In bow tie and knickers
Hull House band playing soft,
sweet notes at dances,
amusement parks and picnics
Benny blowing
bleating
breathing
music
into Benny's clarinet

Summer vacation in Detroit
Hot outside, hotter inside
the Graystone Ballroom
No records
Only real, live jazz
McKinney's Cotton Pickers
and Fletcher Henderson
notes rippling and rumbling
onto the dance floor,
out into the streets
into Teddy's piano

Midway Gardens
Rendezvous Café
The Blackhawk
Benny's clarinet blew
Into town/West Side, South Side, downtown
And out again
All sweet
All dance
All white
All the way to New York

Louis Armstrong loved him
Art Tatum taught him
On the road with
The Lawrence "Speed" Webb band
Teddy tickled the keys in Texas
In Nebraska
In Louisiana
All hot
All rhythm
All black
All the way to New York

Only late at night
In jam sessions
In recording sessions
In Harlem
Offstage, backstage
On vinyl
Were black and white together
When Benny's music swung
with the best
Fast fingering
Drums thumping
Trumpets trumping
It wasn't soft
It wasn't black
It wasn't sweet
It wasn't white
It was swing

And then Benny met Teddy
In Forest Hills, New York
Just for fun
They played
Cool, mellow jazz
"We were thinking
with the same brain,"
said Benny
When his clarinet
And Teddy's piano
Blended into one beautiful
Melody
First they talked
Next they planned
Finally they recorded
"After You've Gone"
"Body and Soul"
"Someday Sweetheart"
With Gene Krupa on drums
On records they became
the Benny Goodman Trio

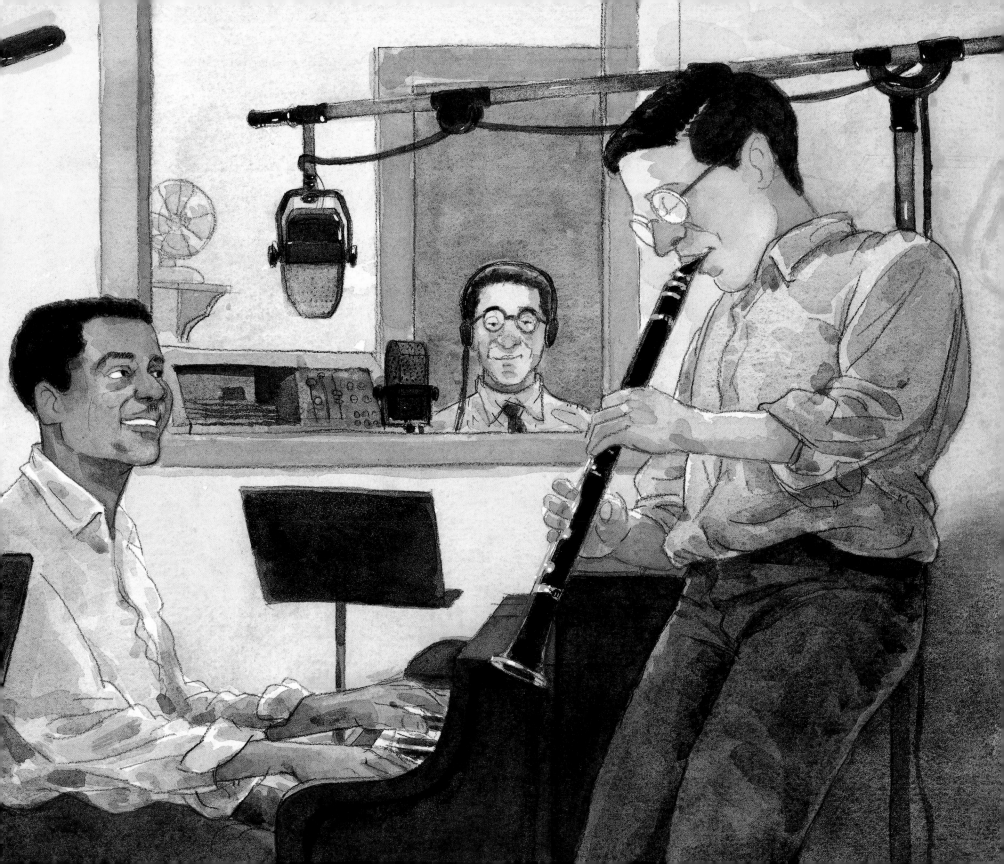

In front of audiences
The trio went on
without Teddy
Audiences weren't ready
For a black-and-white band
But finally Benny said yes
Not to be brave
Not to be bold
"We just did it," said Benny
For the first time ever
Black and white together
"The three of us,
as if we had been born
to play this way."
The audiences were ready
And they stayed,
and they grew,
and they cheered
for the band they heard
on records
for the *original*
Benny Goodman Trio

**Congress Hotel,
Chicago, 1936**

Now onstage, front stage
Playing as one
With Lionel Hampton
on vibraphone
A trio grew
Into a quartet
Drum and vibes
Clarinet and piano
Gene and Lionel
Benny & Teddy
together

"Sing, Sing, Sing"
"Moonglow"
"Memories of You"
Teddy bowed low
Fingers tiptoeing across the keys
Trumpet-style piano
Octaves on his right
Harmony on his left

Benny's clarinet high
Blowing looong, then quick
Blowing loooong, then quick
While Lionel's vibraphone
echoed in back and Gene swept in the bass drum
Tapping in time
all ears
all eyes
Benny watching, listening
Directing
"Drum solo"
"Piano break! Four bars!"
"You take the next chorus!"

Up first was Benny
then Teddy
in came Gene and Lionel
they blew
they tapped
they banged
they strummed
The stage was hot
The dance floor was hotter
The music was hottest

Partners spun and swayed
in and out
Together, apart
And back around
All over the dance floor
Pop boom
Tweet drum
Black, blues
Hot, rhythm
Now it was swing

More about Benny Goodman and Teddy Wilson

Benjamin "Benny" Goodman, aka "The King of Swing," was born in Chicago, Illinois, on May 30, 1909, to Jewish immigrants David and Dora Goodman. Benny was the ninth of twelve children. His father worked as a tailor and later at a stockyard, and the family was extremely poor. When his father heard that a neighbor child earned money playing in a band, he thought it would be a great opportunity for his boys, so he took them to the Kehelah Jacob Synagogue where free lessons and instruments were offered.

Benny immediately took to the clarinet and practiced every day. His father scraped together fifty cents each week to pay his teacher, Franz Schoepp, a classically trained German musician. Schoepp was also one of the only private teachers in Chicago who taught black musicians as well as white. Early on, Benny met influential jazz musicians Jimmie Noone and Buster Bailey through Schoepp. Benny's biggest musical influences were clarinetists Leon Rappolo of the New Orleans Rhythm Kings, Ted Lewis, and Johnny Dodds.

By the time he was a freshman in high school, Benny was performing throughout the city, making more than fifteen dollars a night, more than his father made all week. He often worked so late playing in nightclubs that he was too tired to get up for school in the morning. He eventually quit school at age fourteen.

Benny traveled the country extensively, often switching bands for better pay or for a better opportunity to play music he loved. As a result, from early in his career, he performed with a large variety of musicians, many of whom went on to become jazz greats, such as Bix Beiderbecke, Jimmy McPartland, Tommy Dorsey, Bud Freeman, and Jack Teagarden.

In June 1934, Benny put together his own band and began to play on the nationally broadcasted NBC radio program *Let's Dance!* That same year, he attended a party at the home of vibraphonist Red Norvo and his wife, jazz singer Mildred Bailey, in Forest Hills, New York. There he met a young pianist named Teddy Wilson. The hosts suggested the two play together, and everyone in attendance agreed it was the most magical duo they'd ever heard. Benny declared the experience a "real kick." Jazz promoter John Hammond brought them, along with drummer Gene Krupa, into a recording session, and together they turned out the hits "After You've Gone" and "Nobody's Sweetheart" as the Benny Goodman Trio. However, when it came to taking their act to the stage, Benny was reluctant to introduce an interracial band, fearing it would affect his musical career negatively. Onstage he used pianist Jess Stacey to play the hits the trio had recorded. When the original trio did not appear onstage, patrons walked out, demanding a refund.

With coaxing from promoter Helen Oakley, Benny first played onstage with Teddy Wilson at the Congress Hotel in Chicago on April 12, 1936.

Theodore "Teddy" Wilson was born on November 24, 1912, in Austin, Texas. When he was six, his parents, James Augustus Wilson and Pearl Shaw, moved to Tuskegee, Alabama, to accept teaching positions at Tuskegee Institute. There his father headed the English department and his mother taught reading. Teddy and his older brother, Gus, grew up on the college campus of Tuskegee; and as a teenager, Teddy attended Tuskegee and Talladega College, where he studied piano. In 1931, Teddy moved to Chicago and played with Jimmie Noone, Erskine Tate's Vendome Orchestra, and Louis Armstrong. Through the 1930s and 1940s, Teddy was the music director for singer Billie Holiday and recorded "What a Little Moonlight Can Do" and "Gloomy Sunday." In 1938, Teddy, along with the rest of the members of the Benny Goodman Quartet, performed to a sold-out audience at Carnegie Hall.

Teddy and Benny parted ways in 1940 when Teddy went on to form his own band with saxophonist Ben Webster and trumpeter Shorty Baker. In the 1960s, Benny and Teddy reunited to tour in Russia and appeared at the Newport Jazz Festival in 1973.

"America is the whole world," Teddy once wrote of his experience playing with the first integrated band.

And the rest is history.

Time Line

1817	The earliest form of jazz music is said to have originated in Congo Square, New Orleans, with newly arrived slaves from Africa performing a mix of African and European musical traditions.
1901	Louis Armstrong is born.
May 30, 1902	Benjamin "Benny" Goodman is born to David and Dora Goodman, Chicago, Illinois.
November 24, 1912	Theodore "Teddy" Wilson is born to James Augustus Wilson and Pearl Shaw in Austin, Texas.
1912	Benny begins taking clarinet lessons at Kehelah Jacob Synagogue.
1913	The word *jazz* first appears in print.
1917	The Original Dixieland Jazz Band records "Livery Stable Blues," the first jazz recording.
1918	Teddy and his family move to Tuskegee, Alabama, where his parents teach at Tuskegee Institute and Teddy begins his music education.
1921	Nineteen-year-old Benny makes his professional debut at a Chicago theater.
1926	Teddy begins taking keyboard lessons.
1926	Benny makes his record debut with Ben Pollack.
1929	After majoring in music theory at Talladega College, Teddy leaves Alabama for Detroit to become a jazz musician.

1930	Benny begins performing with the Nichols Band and recording for radio broadcasts. Lionel Hampton plays his first vibraphone solo and makes it his main instrument.
1931	Teddy tours with Louis Armstrong's band.
1933	Billie Holiday makes her first recording.
1934	Benny performs on the NBC show *Let's Dance!*
1935	Benny meets Teddy in Forest Hills, Queens, at the home of jazz artists Mildred Bailey and Red Norvo. Shortly after meeting, Benny and Teddy, along with Gene Krupa, record "Body and Soul," "After You've Gone," "Who?", and "Someday Sweetheart" as the Benny Goodman Trio.
1936	The Benny Goodman Trio performs on Easter Sunday at the Congress Hotel in Chicago, Illinois, making history as the first interracial band to perform publicly.
1936	Lionel Hampton joins the group as vibraphonist to form the Benny Goodman Quartet, and they record "Moonglow."
1964	The quartet reunites to record the album *Together Again!*
1998	The Benny Goodman Quartet receives the Grammy Hall of Fame Award for "Moonglow."

Who's Who in Jazz?

Louis Armstrong (1901–1971) Considered one of the greatest jazz musicians of all time. His influence impacted musicians and vocalists for generations. He got his start in music playing cornet for the Colored Waifs' Home, where he had been sent after a brush with the law, but later switched to the trumpet. He left his hometown of New Orleans for Chicago, New York, and Europe to perform with numerous bands. He recorded the hits "Hello, Dolly!", "What a Wonderful World," and "A Kiss to Build a Dream On." His unrivaled vocals and stage personality led to many film roles.

Johnny Dodds (1892–1940) Self-taught clarinetist from New Orleans who joined Louis Armstrong's Hot Five band.

Edward "Duke" Ellington (1899–1974) Composer, bandleader, arranger, and pianist from Washington, D.C., Ellington, nicknamed the "Duke" as a child because of his royal bearing, carried the name with him throughout his career. He and his orchestra headlined at the famous Cotton Club in New York City's Harlem neighborhood for many years. His "Mood Indigo" recording was inducted into the Grammy Hall of Fame. "It Don't Mean a Thing" and "Stormy Weather" are just two of his many hit songs.

Lionel Hampton (1908–2002) Born in Louisville, Kentucky, Hampton was one of the first jazz vibraphone players. He worked with Buddy Rich, Charlie Parker, Quincy Jones, and Benny Goodman. In 1930, he was hired by Louis Armstrong's band; and in 1936, he joined the Benny Goodman Trio. In 1940, he left Goodman to form his own band, the Lionel Hampton Orchestra, and recorded his most popular hit, "Flying Home."

Fletcher Henderson (1897–1952) Bandleader, arranger, composer, and pianist, Henderson was the son of a piano teacher and a high school principal. He left his native Georgia to pursue a degree in science from Columbia University in New York City and supported himself by playing music. He went on to form one of the most influential and prolific black bands of the 1920s. His orchestra was the predecessor of many swing bands that followed.

Earl "Fatha" Hines (1905–1983) Considered one of the all-time great pianists, Hines influenced Teddy Wilson, Jess Stacy, and Nat King Cole with his unique style of playing with his left hand. "West End Blues" and "Basin Street Blues" were two of his most popular songs.

Gene Krupa (1909–1973) He popularized drum solos, which were rare before Krupa performed his in the swing classic "Swing, Swing, Swing." He played with the Benny Goodman Trio for several years before leaving to start his own group, the Krupa Orchestra.

Jimmie Noone (1895–1944) A New Orleans clarinetist who learned at age fifteen from the great Sidney Bechet.

Art Tatum (1909–1956) Born nearly blind, Tatum was primarily self-taught. Known for his speed and complex rearrangements of classics, he played swing, boogie-woogie, and stride piano. Tatum was influenced by Fats Waller. His 1933 recording "Tiger Rag" established him in the world of jazz.

Thomas "Fats" Waller (1904–1943) Harlem-born Waller was the son of a Baptist minister father and a pianist mother. He studied with master stride pianist James Johnson as well as classical pianists Carl Bohm and Leopold Godowsky. An entertainer, vocalist, and composer of many Broadway musicals, Waller injected lighthearted humor into his music, including his "Honeysuckle Rose" and "Ain't Misbehavin'."

Lawrence "Speed" Webb (1906–1944) While studying embalming in the hopes of becoming a funeral director, Webb played for bands near his hometown in Indiana. He worked with a variety of great musicians, including Art Tatum, Teddy Wilson, and Teddy's brother, Gus, on trombone. By the end of the 1930s, he gave up his band to open a chain of successful funeral parlors.

For Phyllis and all of the enduring friendships
that transcend race — L. C-R.

In memory of James Eugene Williams, "Pops."
Thanks for the music. — J. E. R.

Text copyright © 2014 by Lesa Cline-Ransome
Illustrations copyright © 2014 by James E. Ransome
All Rights Reserved
HOLIDAY HOUSE is registered in the U.S. Patent and Trademark Office.
Printed and Bound in November 2013 at Toppan Leefung, DongGuan City, China.
The illustrations were painted in watercolors.
www.holidayhouse.com
First Edition
1 3 5 7 9 10 8 6 4 2

Library of Congress Cataloging-in-Publication Data
Cline-Ransome, Lesa.
Benny Goodman & Teddy Wilson : taking the stage as the first black-and-white jazz band in history / by Lesa Cline-Ransome ; illustrated by James E. Ransome. — 1st ed.
p. cm.
ISBN 978-0-8234-2362-0 (hardcover)
1. Goodman, Benny, 1909-1986—Juvenile literature. 2. Wilson, Teddy, 1912-1986—Juvenile literature. 3. Jazz musicians—United States—Biography—Juvenile literature.
4. Race relations—History—20th century—Juvenile literature. I. Ransome, James. II. Title.
ML3929.C55 2014
781.65092'2—dc22
[B]
2010048154